POETRY MOVEMENT VOLUME II

A poetry Compilation

'Sometimes I show my scars not because of pride,
But to embrace those wounded'

'Under a skin layer of every Gentleman there is an ugly beast without a
face'

-bhekumuzi kubheka

ACKNOWLEDGEMENTS

Special thanks to all the participant/ Artists which contributed, this could have not been done if it weren't for your moral support.
To my family for loving and caring every day.
To my daughter Okuhle whom I love dearly, thank you for being in my life.
Words could not amount the love I have for all those who supported me.

Sincere apologies for any error in this book the fault is all mine.

CONTENTS

28. I never forget
29. Lost
30. Memories often fade
31. Mid-night Beast and the Boy
32. Monkey on the Tree
33. My everything
34. My love is mine
36. Naked soul
37. Next to the crazy God
38. Old Note Book
40. One last hope
41. Only as human beings
42. Out of Reach
43. Picture isn't complete/ puzzled
44. Pyramid Scheme
45. Raw
46. Red Berries
47. Sanity in a cruel world
48. Shadow
49. She looked single
51. Short-changed lives
52. Storms on the Horizon
53. Sweet, sweet sounds
54. Syria
55. Tell me the truth, I promise I won't get mad
57. Tell your Girl
58. The Bars
60. The cry/ The moan
61. The journey
62. The Myth

63. The poison
64. The right time
65. The second fiddle
66. The sound of my people
67. The Wolf and the Moon
68. The world has its fragrance
69. There is a reason
70. There the Devil that stole my Heart
71. To bear a soul
72. To each has its own
73. Trial and Error
74. Twist and Turn
75. Unsolicited
76. What we talked about when we spoke in silence
77. Where is home
78. Wolf Breath
79. Wonders of the Traveler

~POEMS~

20 SECONDS AND COUNTING

The world goes right round.
Dogs bark at the moon
Evil looms all over
The brown leaf has fallen
I wonder when the next summer is.

The world goes right round.
Ducks swim for the shore
Angels turned into stones
Flower has lost its pigment
I wonder when the next summer is.

In a world where people are
zombies'
Lazy for a job interview
Yet stare at the government's eyes
with begging hands,
Contributing nothing new to the
world.

Should I vomit the truth?
Should I puck it within?
Like a troubled child, I don't know
whether to sob for mother's love or
starvation.
Like statue of nelson Mandela they
all have forgotten.
Every twenty seconds the world
stops and stare.

The world goes right round
The wealthy kill the poor
In less than a minute mother nature
stops and stare while its creation dies

A NOTE OF TIME

This is the stem of my mind
Representing my kind.
A writer's life
Written alright.

A note of time.
Speaking within words so potent
Its message uplifting yet remaining unspoken.
As voices screamed in her head
Telling tales of the great writers
Great poets in time.
As the first light hit the first night
Lips to appear a faint smile
In stage so she rhymed.
Charming the crowd
More pale blue than white
To this journey so they ride.

A note of time
A writer's life written alright.
Glowed and light.
Hugged pain
Hugged love.
Knowledge close to her heart.
Living a dream of that one night
In time gazing upon crushed hearts.
Aching souls wishes of love.

A note of time
This is a stem of my mind
Representing my kind
Written alright
Like a note of time.

A CROSS THE SEAS

A cross the cities,
Wet and dry wood.
I love these two countries but I can't stay in them both,
For my dreams and passions I stood,
I want people I love to be happy and I've done
everything I could,
My love has been here since the undergrowth.
Staying for nine months in Africa is somewhat fair,
I've got my whole life there to claim,
Should I bring all the things to wear?
Or should I buy them over there?
The style is really not the same.
I can't stop thinking about it as I lay,
Today I'm going to where the majority will be black,
My Zulu won't struggle today!
Yet people think that should be the way,
Everybody wants me to come back.
I am telling this story with a sigh,
I've always missed home hence,
In the end it's the whole world and I,
From my village it's less travelled by,
I'm different because I make a difference.

AFRICAN WINGS

African wings,
African flies with mighty wings,
Africa dances,
Africa rises throughout the circumstances.
You haven't seen a dance if you haven't seen African dance,
You haven't heard a song if you haven't heard an African song,
You have missed the heart of our art if you've missed that chance,
Welcome to our land where everything is naturally strong.
Don't get me wrong; I am not talking about man-made problems like poverty,
Africa on its own is a home; you can keep your property,
Through the soil of our land, I feel the souls of our people,
Africa is a place where people are welcomed at every table.

African wings,
African flies with mighty wings,
Africa dances,
Africa rises throughout the circumstances.
You haven't seen praise and worship until you go to Africa,
You haven't seen miracles if your feet haven't kissed our land,
We move instinctively to raise the bar and shout, "Africa!"
The Holy Spirit already came down and grabbed Africa by her hand.
Mother Africa carries comfort for her sons and daughters,
In light and in darkness you'll hear the sound of joyful laughter,
Africa teaches you to walk on gold mixed with blood on the same sand,
Africa teaches you to forgive and love people in your land.

Africa sings,
Africa flies with mighty wings,
Africa dances,
Africa rises throughout the circumstances.

AND STILL THE OCEAN CALLED

I fell into the embrace of a love from my past
In Its place I let of a love sure to last
But somewhere in the recess of my mind
There was a sound I could not leave behind
The echo of the waves
Splashing on my soul
The yearning for the sound of your voice
Was something I could not let go?
I thought that maybe I could go back of my hometown
The friends, the family,
Might be enough to keep me around
But yet my emotions were overcome with that California sound
And I knew where I was supposed to be
To be making love to my Shannan Lee
SO I let the hometown girl go
Cause the yearning for Shanna's sweet love
We something I could not let go
The dream of sharing a pacific oceans view
With my beautiful Shannan
Was too strong
To let fade away
I knew in my heart I had to get her back,
Some way
Well now she is mine once again
And never again will a voice from my past win
For I know where I am supposed to be
Spending the rest of my days with Ms. Shannan Lee
Our love is more than fate
It is simply destiny
For I hear the ocean calling much louder now
As I wipe the sweat off my forehead
The tear from my brow
And soon I will be in California,
Exchanging a Wedding vow.

ARISE

Centuries gone by-

Arise
Hey humanness,

Arise
You were not in the past
The present is in need of you
The future should come to us

Arise
Hey humanness,

Arise
Hey humanness,
You are the dawn
Future is the sun
Wickedness, wrongness
Atrocity, animosity
Should become the past
We do not want
The darkness of yesterday

We,
On the present
Should have future

We,
As human beings
Should have light of life
Hey humanness,
Arise

BRIDGE OF A TROUBLED WATER

I think I remember holding her close.
How did we get so lost in this noisy world?
Now I am mopping over her,
Some nights I moan over what we had

As a child of a sun, I often think of her when I am laying on the green grass.
I didn't promise her forever, but I did promise her to try holding on to her for as
long as I could.
I guess heaven had other plans,
Maybe I didn't try hard enough
They said you
"Can't plough on a desert for Mother Nature cursed the land of the dead"
They said
"Curse who dares go there",
Now sleepless nights haunts the soul I sent to fight my battles.
All the bridges that I have burnt lurks for revenge, but there is something that's
killing me,
Bridge of a troubled water keeps visiting me in my dreams, mocking of what once
was now is no more.

The patterns are aren't clear.
The missing piece of our puzzle is niggle on a haystack.
I don't know where we went wrong or if after broken hearts mend soul mates
become lovers again.
I don't know if the Gods were doing an experiment on us or if were being shown
what true love is,
All I know is that I miss her, I miss us.
I don't know how to get her back, if there is a way I would move heaven and
earth.
I don't know how to show my remorse, if there was a way I would cross that
bridge even though there has been a lot of water under it.
Out of all the bridges I've burnt, I know the bridge of a troubled water still stands
for we hadn't spoke at length.

THE BROKEN VASE

I am used to waking up to no sweet messages.
I am used to walking alone at the park,
Feeding ducks by myself.
The vessel makes a lot of noise when it's empty,
I guess that why I moan a lot lately,
I am used to that.
I guess the feeling had grown fonder.
By the door is a broken Vase.
In this bed is a broken heart.
I wonder which broken pieces I should pick up first.

CHEMISTRY

The erupting surge of emotions
Beyond walls of concealment
Pass stature of seriousness
Disrupting one's true senses
It is wires crossed causing a spark
Each time we inches apart
Like a distant thunder that raptures
Without so much sound but lightning
Chemistry is you in me
Invading all my sacred spaces
Defeating all forms of resistance
Hopelessly bending my will without a twist
Chemistry is the unbeaten drums that sounds
The song my heart sings when you call my name
Echoing pass stolen glances
Trailing all me through my silent moments
Chemistry are the burning memories
With our hands glued palm to palm
With not so many words spoken
Yet the silence is filled with assurance
Chemistry is my stirred up emotions
Warmth at the thought of your touch
Shivers at the memory of yester encounters
Chills each time we paste our lips and kiss

CLOUDED

My mind is a cloud
Not tethered
To the conventions of reality.
Floating high above the confines
Of my body
I look down upon those
Who are grounded?
I am a cloud inside the Cloud
Which is like living
In the universal mind
It gets tiresome to know
Everything there is to know.
Here I am never in a fog
Of torpor and dullness
As long as I am
Collecting and categorizing
The random bits of experience
That come my way.
I am proud of my virtual life
As a cloud.
My mind is never clouded.

COCKTAIL STICKS AND STONES

Midnight morns,
Geneva gin, let's begin again.
With a girl on my arm I was spinning her
A yarn because you all know that young men tell lies,
Her eyes held my eyes and melted through to the 'come to bed' lies
And the truth was met in the, 'I'll get the next drink in'
Let's begin again.
The truth,
(Well that's new)
Is we did not do although
I wanted to.
I'm going to meet her on Friday my pay day and....
Take her away to Bexhill on sea,
She'll be delighted.

COLD WET MORNING

You'll only come to the funeral to laugh at me,
But when you look at the plain wood and earth remember this,
You'll soon be joining me,
Remember this,
I was here first.
I was always first.
You never laughed at that,
Did you?
Who's laughing now?

CROWDED MIND

The selfish and the selfless
Have this in common
The crowded mind of the self.
Will my self-sacrifice suffice?
Or do I need the self-realization
Of the selfish?
The pleasure principle
Is a selfish pursuit.
With self-division
Selfish motives become suspect
And altruism wins the day.
A win-win situation
Plays itself out.
The selfless are asleep at the switch.
Never run with a crowd
That doesn't know
Where it's going.

EBB AND FLOW

The ebb and flow of life
Is relentless.
Single minded like the tides
In their pursuit of change.
The abyss takes on a whole new meaning
When you find yourself
On top of the world.
There was never any choice
But to act the part you were assigned
In victory and defeat.
A change in direction
Is part for the course?
When you factor in
The quirks of fate
There was nowhere else to go.
To escape
The highs and lows.

EYE TO EYE

We don't see eye to eye
It seems you don't mind

What clouded your mind?
Wiping off your beautiful smile?

We don't see eye to eye
You've walked far for miles

What tore us apart?
You no longer mine!
Gone are the talks

Am I out of your thoughts?
You so distant and cold
Where is the one I loved?
Can we go back to time?
Or is it too late to try
Did I tell you a lie?

I wish to make amends
We do not see eye to eye

We are worlds apart
Though it breaks my heart
I am not going to cry

FOOLS DIVE IN

A fool for love
Is a fool for pain.
A thing of the heart
Yet so lame.
Danced by few fools insane.
Today you have wings flying up high
Tomorrow you're not the same.
Now you're changing lanes.
Thou with a brokenhearted down to pieces
Even now with another you love fame.
Love forbid for showing off
Distort a human mind
Ignite her silence heart.
Like a flame burning inside.
Only fools dive in love
Get drunk in love.
Sharing hearts like the last slice.
And find no words to rhyme when things get tough.
A feeling deep dismay in crime
Beating for another in time.
Shakes you on your knees
Whenever she walks by.
Blows with wind
And then you lose your mind.
You walk tall
Talk the talk and it's alright.
As lid's and hip's
Eyes lights up than his.
Blinded indeed
Love sick.
Takes your breath away
Like the breeze beyond the sea's.
The soft touch of his lip's
Blocking you seeing the truth in him.

Ghazal

I need to hear your song always
I wish to live very strong always

A spoiled word cannot make sense
Without you I will be wrong always

Willingly I shall mull over you
For efficacy of life I long always

I paint myself only with your thoughts
To the world aesthetic I belong always

Your feelings, drive me to the future
Ecstatically, I will come along always

THE GRASS IS GREENER THIS SIDE

Golden sky's seen even by the blind
Heart weep for love
Of the near far.
That shines brighter than the stars.
His is where the sun comes out not the shine.
But to worship love.
The grass is greener this side
The roots of men go deep in fertile
Where fruits grow
And faces glow.
Here is where you find peace
Knowledge above his
To free yourself from the ignorance cage of this world
Believing not in love but in lust
Marriage to life
To lust and in the end it's complicated.
The grass is greener this side
Here is the garden of hope and life
Love patience and divine
Love medicine sex
We hold on to one rope
In pain and in love.
Leading light to the bleeding hearts.
Marriage life
To the couples in love.
Cheers.

GRAVEYARD ON THE FRONT PORCH

They speak the bone language.
A wild flower grows on their front porch.
They try to read your palm but there are no lines in it,
My child you have been digging.
Startled by the stars, they run to the north desert and came back empty handed
Who's forbidden life on this planet?
Dare they ask?
While a wild flower grows on their front porch.
Isn't it the blood they spilled?
Isn't it there deceit?
Killed the résistance of pure heart just to fulfill their evil ways
Dare I ask about the white crosses on the front porch?
The answer to the question in my mind was
"Surveyors had come to cross their land"
Once again a victim of a kind heart was me.

HEART OUT OF REACH

Dear heart of mine,
I wish you had eyes.
I wish you had hands.
Limbs of a mind.
Sometimes I wish I can take you off this poor body of mine.
Sometimes I wish I can reach out to you and mend you.
Maybe one day I will understand why you're always out of reach
Maybe one day you will see who loves you and who doesn't.
Maybe think for a while before you bite bate.
It pains me to know I can never see you
It hurt so much to know that you are here,
And that we always speak but will never get to meet
Sure mountains will never come to a cross road
Sometimes I look in the mirror and hope that I see you.
Dear heart of mine
Oh how I love you
If only you weren't out of reach

HEARTLESS

Upon shattered pieces
You walk tall with pride
Your face is fanned by their tears
Through their pain excitement you
ignite

You beat your chest
Tell the world you the best
But your day is fast approaching
Will you stand your share of pain?
Oh heartless player
You've caused lakes of tears
Upon a pile of broken heart pieces
You stand tall without shame!

Why pay love with hurt
Why this thorny wall of defense
Don't you too long to be loved
What if you lose the best of loves?
Player change your ways
Before fate comes your way
With vengeance to rip you apart
To pay you back for all the harm

THE GOOD SON

I am his son.
He carry me.
When I was weak,
He loves me.
When no one does,
I will love him.
I will shelter him.
I will carry him.
In his ailing moment,
I will be his light,
I will be his sunrise.
In his darkest nights.
I will love him.
I will not trade him,
For any wealth or riches.
He is my only one.
My good father.
I will him forever,
Because...
I am his good son.

I AM TIRED

There are days where I hold my breath for a very long time.
There are nights where I sink my head in to the bottom till I suffocate.
There are times where I close my eyes with both hands and open my fingers just
to see little,

There are those days where my eyelashes just shut them self-down for a very
long time for no reason.
Days where I cut myself just to see if I still bleed.
The brute I cause within is severe.

I am tired
I feel naked in front of a crowed I know not.
My pride has fallen
My ego flew away and didn't look back
NOAH and the white Dove
Jesus and the crumbs

Some nights I drive through the desert hoping to come back with something
Some nights I just want to cuddle and lay in bed all day
I heard a child wishing for rain
I couldn't careless
My scars are deep,
My teeth has sunk rock bottom,
But how am I supposed to say I am tired?

I AM

I am
Changing,
Into someone I've never known before,
Another year older,
Body a little more sore.

I am
Another year wiser,
From experiences learned,
From times of promise,
Times I have been burned

I am
Striving
Learning
To become more caring
Understanding

I am
Simply changing
Into the life I was meant to lead
I am simply trying to be the best I can be

I am
Loving
Caring
Trying to be kind
Sharing

I am
Just me
I am a man trying to fulfill my destiny

I am
Human
Making a mistake or two

I am learning not to hold onto frustration
But simply stepping back to take a different view

I am
Perhaps even learning a thing or two

I am
Human
No different than you
I am, Just me.

I LOVE YOU BETTER NOW

 I really love you so much
Better now, the two of us
Are safer, we have pushed
The tide away, and are so
Much closer to the coast

I really love you better now
That our lost love is a ghost
Our new love, is so much better
We chose love to be our host
Our lives are full of challenges

Our forgiveness beats out greed
No room left here for emptiness
For true love is all that we need
Well some love, can last forever
While some love, it lasts a while

I'm praying to the angels of love
That I will forever make you smile
I know that in our troubled past
Well something's were so bitter
Something's were so great, some not so
It's entirely up to us loving better

Now it's time to bury negativity
When we feel our love is true
I crave you as a little part of me
I know you're craving for me too
You know you have me ready

Since that night I fell for you
If you are really are a believer
Then someday, you'll say "I do"

I LOVED SOMEONE ELSE'S

How could I stoop so low?
Like a child with a toy on one hand,
But wants another on the other.
Like a moon blocking the sun on a daylight
I loved someone else's wife while mine waited at home with kids.
I loved someone else's house while mine was the state of art,
And they lived in a shack.
They say a heart speaks volume
They claim a body is a slave of a mind
That you can't have your cake and eat it
I was happy with her, rather than with her
She was my amusement park
My full moon
She was everything to me
Until her husband caught us and shot her

I NEVER FORGET

I never fought in no war
Did not die
What the fuck for?
So...
Some future generation could piss on my grave?
Graffiti my gravestone?
Smash my home?
Take my wife?
No.
I did not fight in no war.
What the fuck
Would I do that for?

LOST

I missed those moments
When I am with you
When our hearts was still surrounded with love
No lies
No deceits
Now, everything changed
All hate and regrets.....
I still miss you.

MEMORIES OFTEN FADE

As wounds heal
Scars remain
Memory often fade

Before the rising sun kisses a new day,
A can of warms has been opened.
Before the sun goes back home and the dogs of the night comes out to play,
The grim reaper hunts my soul.
The white whale hunts baby seals on their ponds.
Before collecting sea shells in the middle of the night, witches test their
new spells

The moon is always round, yet I have forgot the sound of an empty vessel
The sun is always burning, I no longer know the back of my hand
The memory often fade

As wounds heal
Scars remains
Memory often fade

The kiss once longed for, dead and gone
Hugs once cherished gone with the wind
Blur pictures on the mind like the seal who had forgotten about its pups.

MID-NIGHT BEAST AND THE BOY

Son of the morning,
Out for a night to dance
The rod is ready
The aim is clear as the blue skies
The hunter becomes the hunted

The moon has shown the other side of its face
The sea haul for war that's about to take place
Grass sees like regale snakes
Boat so slow like a snail on the wall
Don't rock the boat worms for tonight you're the bait

Don't blink twice in this vast waters
Or you will swallowed alive.
Like puppets dancing to the sound of the drums beat
It's the currency against the boat
The beast shows its ugly face opening its evil eye
It's a dangerous dance

MONKEY ON THE TREE

Swinging from right to left
Swinging from left to right
Swing, swing
        Monkey on the tree what do you want?

Monkey on the tree mourn, the jungle mourns.
Monkey on the tree jumping up and down on the branches

        Monkey on the tree what do you want?

Swaying from right to left
Leaping from left to right
I gave you candy but you threw it away
I gave you chips but you cast it away
Now all I am left with is this banana

        Monkey on the tree what do you want?

        Jumping up and down on the tree.

MY EVERYTHING

My heartbeat
My joy

My moon and the stars
Mother of my world
My piece of heaven on earth
I loved you before my birth
Surely you grow in my mind
Planted by him who cannot be seen?

My love song
I sing till I lose my breathe
Your voice warms up my heart.
My dream come true
To my core you cut.
My green and blue
So I stick to you.
Your worth is beyond my word

I owe it to you.
Palm of my hand
My rip
Forever you I keep.
My tree of dreams.
You're like the moon
Glamour I cannot reach.
I see you coming towards me
Even though you're deeply rooted in the earth

In spirit you are rich.
I know where you have been
Still your leaves are green
The give me life to live.

MY LOVE IS MINE

My love is mine
Mine only
To be thrown back to my face every time.
My love is deep
So me true and still.
My love is shy
Humble and kind.
My love is sweet
Precious and for real.
To be thrown back to my face every time.
My love from within
I love you and I mean it.
From the bottom of my heart I feel it.
To be thrown back to my face every time.
My love is mine
Mine only to be thrown back to my face every time.
My love is tough
Fair... I call it like I like
Because I don't care
And you cannot make me care.
To be thrown back to my face every time.
My love is dangerous
Crazy madly in love
Uncontrollably like a sickness inside.
My love is unforgivable
Unforgettable
You broke my heart my trust and my love
And I don't need you in my life
Don't want to see my love.
To be thrown back to my face every time.
My love is disappointed
Will never be truthful
Not caring a game
We are just playing
To be thrown back to my face every time.

My love is mine
Mine only to be thrown back to my face every time.
My love is pain
I've been hurts
I've been insane.
I've cried so many times and my broken heart
Cannot take it
Please don't start. Be gentle with me by your side.
On my knees be giving
Because to give me you won't be receiving.
To be thrown back to my face every time.
My love is b....! You mine
No one will ever love you like me... You mine
Not your mama
Not your daddy
Especially not you.
Not when I'm still alive.
To be thrown back to my face every time
My love is mine
Mine only to be thrown back to my face every time.
My love is babe... I'm sorry
I didn't mean to hurt you
I live without you
Please forgive me
Now I said I'm sorry what are sulking for...
Because without me you're nothing
You know you need me
To be thrown back to my face every time.
My love is I know what you want
I've been here before so many times
Since I was a child.
So be it... take as you like.
Because all you do is take from me every time.
My love is mine
Mine and mine only
To be thrown back to my face every time.

NAKED SOUL

I am naked
I stripped everything in me
Including my pride

I surrendered
My lost self as I renew my vows
I will walk in your kingdom

Selfless, coated
With humility
Free from deceit and lies

I am coated with self-belief
That the world I chose,
Is the world free from the dark?

One big leap
For a change of heart
Form a dark one
To a golden heart.

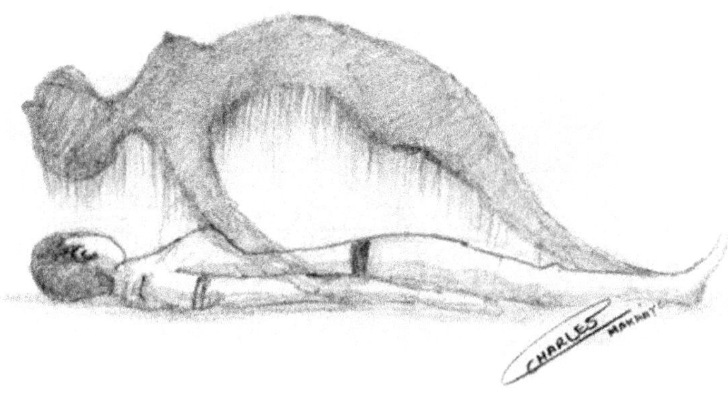

NEXT TO THE CRAZY GOD

From a far I heard a priest yelling
"I can help you son"
From a far I turned and look
I felt disgusted.
I felt empty.

The chemistry and the fume
This world is a lab
The Gods set out tests and run experiments'
Was I ever created for a purpose?
Or was I an error on the formula?

From a far I heard the priest yelling
"I can help you son"
From a far I turned and look
And all I saw was a businessman
The church as a business
While the Gods were busy chasing Lab Rats

THE OLD NOTEBOOK

Monday,
Unpacking today
Memories of my past come into play
In an old notebook I had stored away
Notes I had written of feelings of love

From a not so distant past
Letters to and from and old love
That I thought was going to last
Reminding me that sometimes some loves
Just aren't meant to be

So as my bag was packed,
So has my heart moved on?
Step by step

Like an old typewriter on auto Correct
She lies somewhere tonight thinking,
I am sure of me
But I have found a new love
Who treats me blissfully?

For time she did
But after awhile
It was all but gone
Now her notes will be wadded up
And thrown away

Just as the old notebook was once stored
In the old suitcase
As the memories
Will forever be stored somewhere in the vast spaces?
Of my mind and heart

And with this new love
I soon will begin a new life
A new start
As I pray she finds love again someday
And like me,
She is able to put our memories of our time together away

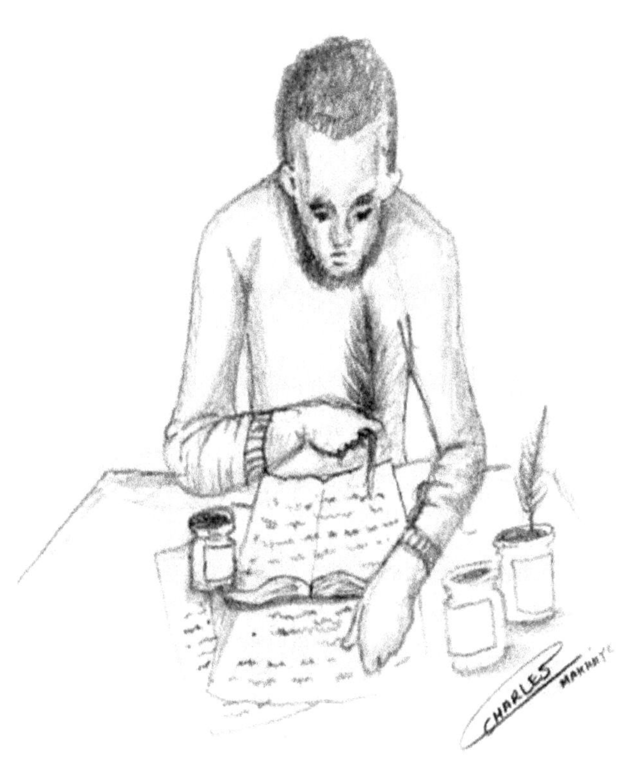

ONE LAST HOPE

Like sand through the hour glass,
I am counting.
Like white birds of heaven,
I fly high.

People judge each other like its judgment day.
People fail to try.
How can I blame them?
Failure is within

.

Like a grain of sand in a grass I try to play my part.
Like animals we discriminate....
He who can't eat with them.
She who can't play with them.
They who can't sit, cause of the pigment.
Them whom shall not speak nor voice out, cause of their sexuality.
Failure is within.

Remember failure is within.
Since when being gay meant war?
Since when being a lesbian meant exactions?
Cast on a land of unknown cause of our sexuality.
Cast out for our true colors,
I still fly above the clouds.
In my dreams I still surf above the wave of dehumanizing humanity for their
sexuality
I pray one day my dream will come true.

ONLY AS HUMAN BEINGS

While you and I make a fusion
Failing not we should have fruition

As we people are very many
Importantly we must have harmony

At any time we can be corrected
To each other we must get connected

In the space between you and I
Menace should be erased
As we stay in our place
With peace we should be graced

Living safely is living greatly
Living humbly is living honorably

Let us get out of wrongness
Let us get in to rightness

We have been born as human beings
We must die only as human beings

OUT OF REACH

Nearly within expanding grasp
Not very far away within reach
Stranded again so alone and lost
Wishing I were on a sunny beach

The grain of sand so amazing
In the warm sand all is not well
The shadow cast upon the sea
As I look around the seas swell

As I try to capture all of them
The waves crash against beach
I try so very hard catch them
All these waves are out of reach

Yes so very far out of reach
Simply have no chance anymore
No cannot catch crashing waves
As they crash and hit the shore

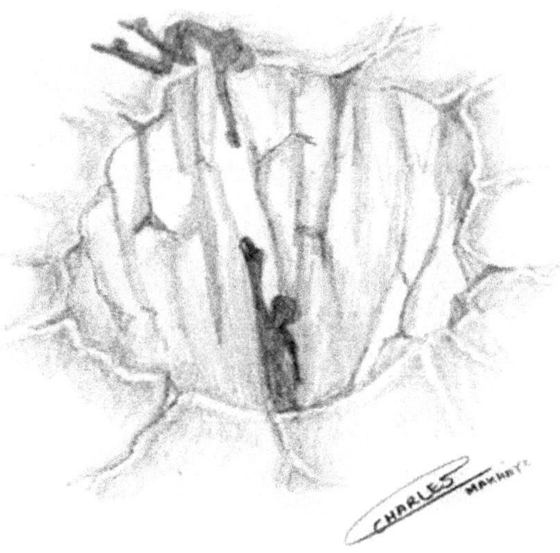

As they are slipping and sliding through my jaded voice I preach slipping further
And further away
From these tides of sands reach
Out of reach here on this beach
Asking myself how will I manage?

 As I look back towards the shore
All that I can see is the carnage
Left behind like a ship wrecked
By the emergence of the water
Standing here alone once more
I, a mere lamb to the slaughter

THE PICTURES ISN'T CLEAR/ PUZZLED

I try to visualize it with my eyes closed,
All I see is the youth becoming zombies walking in slow-motion and talking in vain,
 Barely hearing the meaning behind the lazy voice.
Blue skies shifting but clouds standing still
The picture isn't complete.
I try to paint it with rainbow colors but it remains black and white
I see vultures preparing for their next feast, a lonely soul in the desert.
Young blood killing everything it's fearing including their own souls.
Roads like snakes that swallows everything that walks in its path.
The man in power keeps laughing at funerals, I guess the income is good.
The picture isn't complete.
We expected rain drops at the party but floods showed,
How amusing.
The mocking bird keeps singing inside the cage
My neighbor's curtain keeps waving at me.
I mixed the colors to see what it would make,
I closed my eyes for a very long time and try to picture you smiling
A prose is missing in our poem
A picture missing a mark of a beast won't sell.
Goodness comes when least expected
How could you be so blind not to see the devil next door?
Blue jeans and sweat T-shirt he walks alone in my picture, missing,
A friend or two.
The picture isn't complete
Kids playing in the park and heaven opening its gates for us
Like a puzzle missing a piece, I miss you.
They say we don't know what we got till it's gone
Picture isn't complete until you stand far from it
Only than the ugly reveals its beauty
Something is missing.

PYRAMID SCHEME

Far from the ocean it rose
Shining like gold
OH-African child
You fell for it

Far from the internet it tempted your soul,
Like a child watching pornography
You never wanted to sleep.
A flower that lost its pigment whilst blooming.

All the dime exchange
Lost on the flowing river
OH-African child
Now all is lost
Gone with the wind.

Its eye hypnotized you
Its apex sucked blood from your vain.
Your sweat gone in vain
Loan shark knocking on the door to collect what's
left
Children are starving looking at you in the eyes.

Raw

The mud is still young
The concrete is wiser and strong
But the construction workers are weary
They are connoisseur of mud
The steel covered by rust.
It has been ages,

Yet nickel and dime on their pockets.
Consolidating its bands and corners.
They will probably never driver on these roads.
They will probably never live on these building,
Nor will they get to bask on the sea shore they had built.
All their hard work goes in vain with pennies on their raw rough hands

Skin pale like cement
Hands strong like steel

Concealing an incorruptible future for the young blood,
While it drowns on the pool of pointless substances.
They barely remember their children's name
They are like soldiers on camps

The older they are, the better they work says their masters.
No Street will be named after them like politicians.
No building will be built in memory of their hard works.
Their feelings had gone rogue no remuneration
Just a raw mud waiting.

RED BERRIES

Red berries summer fruit flavor
Cold to taste on a toddlers lips

As he is drinking from the bottle
So joyfully drinking as he gulps

Laughing loud hands on head
Oh the sight of something funny
Cuddling a little cut toy doggy
Poor I, thinking it was a bunny
Shrieking out loudly with delight

As we are running together fast
Flying down this steep escalator
And making this fun totally last
Next up, he's sitting in a toy bus

I am rocking it and it is shaking
In his mind he is the only driver

Not just driving, but actualizing
Safely strapped in his car seat

Munching on a packet of crisps
Again drinking a red berry drink

Giving me high five funny gasps
As he waves to me his goodbye
Blowing me loving little kisses
With his fingers held to his lips
Granddad, yes I how we miss us.
See you soon Ryan

SANITY IN A CRUEL WORLD

Clown giggling at your tears.
Crowed don't recognize your face any more.
All your sweat gone in vain
Invading the soul with their instrumental music
Dangle your arms and feet to the grave.

Stop.
When the bad news came I felt sick
Then they putted their fingers on my thoughts.
My tongue stuck out like a dog
Begging for food
A long bearded man with a collar shouting the end is near
I think I am going to be sick again.

Stop.
When will this all stop?
Children are being raped and silenced with candy.
Adult are being raped and silenced with money.
Like slaves in the past I will do anything for food
Riot on all corners of the world.
Havoc within the mind
Tell me to jump, I only ask how high?
Like a slave I beg of you to punish me for no reason

Stop.
It's a bad world out there
I feel cannibalism near then the world expected
It's a crying shame for those who doesn't know how sanity feels.

SHADOW

Shadow your shadow
Until you know the night.

Take refuge in your memories of light.
They will show the way
Out of the cave.

Darkness is an ally of furtive movements
Find out where it goes.

At the gates of perception
You may pass unchallenged
To the underworld.

Where you will meet the foe
You thought you knew
Wrapped in the mantle of night.

Do nothing with your terror
Of being exposed
In a light that is no light
Of this world.
A light that knows.

SHE LOOKED SINGLE

She sat across the room surrounded by golden chairs of royalty.

She resembled royalty
She looked lonely and in need of a company
Her eyes kept dancing according to the sway of her hands
She played around with her fingers
Her fingers kept playing around her chest and neck
The gentlemen across the room created sweet fantasies
They played melodically tunes that were produced by fat wallets
Expensive cellphones complemented by gadgets
They kept talking pictures with their mind frames of thought
Her eyes kept being synchronized with a wordographer who was taking
Word pictures of the situation
Across the room

She was making it a point to capture his attention
She changed her point to capture his attention
She changed her posture after she realized
He wasn't looking at her,
Little did she know?
His eyes were capturing her every move
Through the reflection of the glass door

So he kept capturing reflections
She made a greater effort
She started to moan and groan
That finally got his attention
He turned around, he smiled
Then he looked back down to the pieces of serviette

He was writing on
Her beauty made many want to travel
As they marveled
The men tour on her surface with their eyes
One brave soldier finally decided to stand up and approach her
He moved across the golden chairs

Went over the mountain looking eyes
Peeking out of the room
He almost tripped over the broom
He was quick to imagine himself as he groom
So he decided to propose on the spot
To a woman he has only seen from across the room
His attempt was declined

She asked why me?
He replied you look single
So she than asked: so do you propose to all the single woman you meet
Actually I'm wrong we haven't met
So you propose to woman you have only seen across the room
She chased him away
She kept wondering what the guy in the corner was writing
She looked single

Until a well-built man walked into the room
He went straight to her table and kissed her
The so called gentlemen got angry
She stood up and she only had one leg

The fat wallets and big gadgets were put back in the bags
The guy with the ring ran away
Why do they run when they see such?
She is the same woman they saw before
She is beautiful and sexy
She was able to make them wet their pants
Just by looking at them
She is a woman like all others
She is able to turn heads with her confidence.
She looked single...

SHORT-CHANGED LIVES

I grew up in Africa short-changed,
Wealth exchanged by coins,
Cows killed remained unchanged,
"School fees for everyone joins"

Unreturned investments from people,
Too much to give, ended up in deficit,
"Poor investments", business people,
Still giving when nothing is definite.

Cars can be changed like shoes,
Clothes can be changed like coins,
Houses making headlines in the news,
Kids showing kindness by collecting cans.

Silence becomes a friend to the owed,
People fight for their return until they are tired,
They give much and remain with a heavy load,
Troubling inflation with people hardly hired.

Real change begins with a good heart,
That's the only place that really matters,
Change your heart, change your life if you're smart,
Changed hearts equal real people not actors.

If life has made you bitter,
If hurts have made you hard,
Clean heart is your life's best guard.

If your storms remained unchanged,
If you have invested more than you got back,
If your storms remained unchanged.
You're about to get more than you've ever invested back.

STORMS ON THE HORIZON

The storms on the horizon
They are just like the poison

Which some killers try to ploy
I promise, I tell no word of a lie
Are church goers really forgiven?
With some killers still sinning

Living life is sometimes dull
An unneeded excitement cull

And sometimes lackluster
Though it can be clustered
When completely surrounded
Especially when it is protected
By media, by veils and by collars

Expensive fancy suits and ties
All these uniforms of distinction

All bought with formal education
Reverend spelt backwards

Is "Dnerever" how interesting?
Now, please take a note
No, I don't have the antidote
Is this writing making any sense?

 Maybe, I am liking the suspense
Does it make sense in a world?
 That we only think we know
Or do we just agree anyway
Our minds pondering to and fro
How interesting as only you know.

SWEET, SWEET SOUND

The most beautiful voice echoed their ears,
The sweet, sweet sound of the gentle melody,
It knocked their feet and dried their tears,
It touched their souls and became their remedy.

They swayed in time as they became one with the sound,
Caught up in the moment only music they could hear,
All of a sudden the beat dropped down on the ground,
They all became one like the three musketeers.

There was swinging, tapping and clapping in the room,
Everybody shouted the same name,
They smelled the aroma of the sweet perfume,
Their lives were never the same.

They became more alive during the rise of the tempo,
Shaking of the dust they adopted from earth,
They recognized the calmness of that echo,
It was from before the foundations of the earth before their birth.

Amazing music that needed no manuscript,
It carried them to the sky of wonders,
This new life had no overanalyzed transcript,
The songs dropped down like rain in countless numbers

SYRIA

It's a worrier
And
No wonder I can't sleep.
Do we stay out or,
Do we go in with 'boots on the ground?'
Harold said,
'This won't affect the pound in your pocket'
That's torn it,
The hawks will have orgasms,
But no win, no fee or should that be,
No win, no free?
It's a puzzle of a poser,
Suppose we dispose of the lies,
We could with an open pair of eyes see things differently.
I think infantry,
In my infancy I fancy
There's always a chance we might stay out.

TELL ME THE TRUTH I PROMISE I WON'T GET MAD

I can't continue living a lie.

Be honest with me
I know you're afraid to loose me, but you won't.
If you don't tell me the truth you might.
I already know the truth
Just confirm it.

We can get through this if we meant too.
We have gone through a lot of shit together
Near death experiences we've shared
Past scars we've helped each other heal

It's sad to live a lie
Disguised as the truth
I know I seem perfect but I am not, I have many flaws
So please tell me the truth, I promise I won't get mad.

I've told you before I've connected with your mind.
I know what goes on in that head of yours
I know you more than you think I know.

I'm an I.T specialist.
I'm good at bending technology rules.
I can find anything I want on the cyberspace.
I choose not to.

Because I trust you will tell me the truth.
Don't be afraid to.
You are sometimes my weakness
Just make sure you know what you are doing.
Make sure you don't dress up the truth with
"I don't want to hurt him excuses"

I deserve to know
I know you about my flaws

Don't make a mistake of hiding your true feelings.
I'm old enough to see when I'm not being told what I need to know
That bullshit of "what he doesn't know won't hurt him"
Well I am connected to you so it hurts me
Never say you love me when you love the idea of loving me.

When I love, I love dearly
I give in to what I'm given
In return I give in soulfully

Be careful when reading these poetic thoughts.
Not everything is just creative free verse flow.
It's feeling of a real human being
A person who is what most are not
Are you sure you are being honest with me?
I don't doubt your love, I doubt your actions

TELL YOUR GIRL

Tell your girl she is lucky
 She has your time and heart
 She lays her head on your chest
 She softly leans on your shoulder

Tell her to value the love given
 For the same someone else longs
 If she knew she would make you her treasure
 Place you amongst her most valued pieces

Tell your girl there are eyes watching
 Counting on her flaws and ignorance
 What she views as falling crumbs
 Are worth more to someone who lacks

Tell her to hold on to your love
 Never let go of your hand
 Nor let her eye to wander
 For you worth all the attention

I wish to tell your girl these words
 She lives the life someone dreams
 She has the heart someone desires
 She even owns your affection

Someone lacks her happiness
She longs for a fraction of your affection
 Prepared to go miles to return the attention
 Tell your girl to count her blessings

THE BARS

Let me confess.
I was there when he died.
I kept quite when he cried.
I looked in his eyes as he was fried.

When the police came I lied
About my sight of the event that changed my life
It was hard to say exactly how it happened
At first it was about the door I had opened

I went in there with the intention to steal
A few cookies and change so I could give my 2year old son Shintsho (change)
Change?
Yes his name means change

I had never given him anything I'm proud of before.
That had to change.
All he was ever told was that…
'Your father is a good for nothing bastard, who is just a sperm donor'
That was partly true, I had nothing to my name,

No job,
No home,
No income.

Just selling of fruits on the street
To pay for my shelter and water.
Waking up every morning
Pushing the trolley every day,
Given a ticket every day.

The Metro police taking away the only link between my son and me
Making me hate every moment on the street
They confiscated the goods because I didn't have a permit
My pain has caused me to drift away from what I initially got your attention for,
Why?

Why? Why did I open that door?
I wouldn't have witnessed his terrible murder.
He was burnt because he refused to open the empty safe.
Why keep an empty safe?
Why save a cashless safe?

Didn't he think about the insurance?
Why fight to keep safe that can be replaced?
Money has become more valuable than life
The fire in his eyes
Burnt permanent marks in my mind

The fighting spirit he showed he was one of a kind
The kind of a person who believes money is more valuable than his own life.
Don't get me wrong the guy who brutally murder him were wrong,
They were not supposed to take what didn't belong to them.
I confess that I sat behind the shelves.
I watched him die, even when they were out of the store

I was still in shock
But that doesn't justify
I let an innocent man die
Today I stand behind these bars guilty of arson
My fingerprints were all over the man's clothes

A few months before that I went to the post office to get my grant money but my
fingerprints didn't match, I had burnt them during a fire at my shack
Fire was following me like I was petrol.

These flames are stronger than me
I'll continue writing this poem when I can it's too painful to even pour out my
thoughts here behind these bars!

THE CRY/ THE MOUN

I cry,
Not because I am sad.

I cry,
Because free.

I take back my freedom.
Free from being hurt.
Free form oppression.
Free discrimination,
That I am black.
That I am different.
That I am no better than any race
I shed tears,
Because the world now believes in equality
Appreciates me being black
Recognized my beauty
My talent
They listen
To all the words I speak

I cry
Because
Freedom is now mine.

THE JOURNEY

You try
So hard
Changes come
Catch you off guard

You do
All that you can
Just to get by
Whoever said life is easy

Was telling a lie
You never know
Where the paths of life will go
Sometimes the mere foothills you see

Turn into mountains for you and me
But still you push on
Hoping all along
It gets easier
At times it won't
At times it will

It's a testimony of courage
A testimony of sheer will
Life may get crazy but oh what a thrill
So continue to push on
Till all your strength is gone
And your journey is done
For it was life

To be led only by you
And you must not quit
So keep on doing exactly what you have got to do

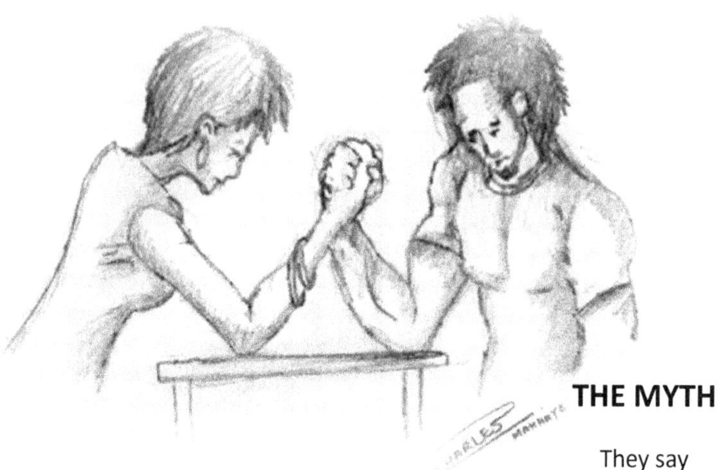

THE MYTH

They say
That the world is fair
That it's crazy and the most stupid words spoken
If the world is fair
There shall be no more beggars all are rich
There shall be no more deceits all kindness
There shall be no more homeless
All are rich politicians and real estate brokers
There shall be no more masters all slaves.
Equality is taboo
Only in these manner we become equal
First, in the eyes of law because the law speaks
That those who are less in life must have more law...
Second in the eyes of God
Because, we are all his sons in his eyes no rich or poor
No strong and weak
But to others
Equality is a myth.

THE POISON

I was poisoned
My body is weakening
My heart is burning with hate
My eyes are loaded with tears

I am dying
Because of the venom of love
My body was paralyzed
As you kissed me goodbye

Too much love
Killed me
I lost air to breath
I lost my will to live

I summoned the goddess
Of love to heal my broken heart
I beg of you
Teach me how to stand up

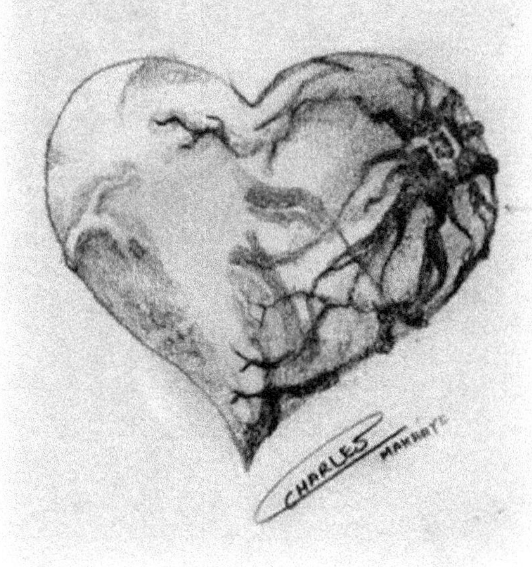

THE RIGHT TIME

Poetry is being searched
Many have learned that

Poets move ahead
They relied upon
Words, sentences and languages

Poets try
Experiments many they do

Without pause
Continue poets
They invite one and all

Welcome you all
This is the right time
We all should read poets
 We all should find out poetry

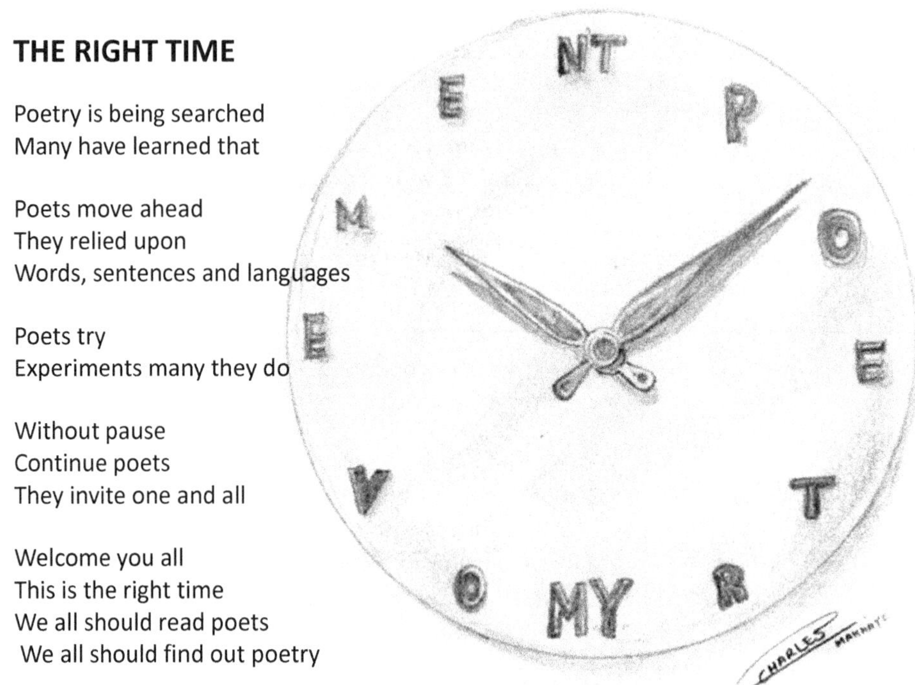

THE SECOND FIDDLE

And the morning washes in to wake me so to pray
Every time I lay these bones of mine to rest they remind me of
Another morning when the time was not so urgent in the pressing of coffee to my
lips
Memories skip lightly behind the lined lids of my eyes
And I am children once again
Looking to the skies and thinking there's no end to this,
I am at the core of my being seeing this being me,
Ageing. Listening to my cantankerous joints squealing and creaking
Ageing. My fears,
Ears that can't hear
No sight when light cannot enter in
 The darkness of eternity
The extremity of space
And the face I look for
The face itself is
The central core,
The morning washes in again
The night rinsed from my hair,
My fears laid bare
My hands are tied.

THE SOUND OF MY PEOPLE

I hear the sound of my people,
Coming from the desert land,
I hear the sound of my people,
Rising from where I stand.

The sound that permeates my soul,
The sound that infiltrates my goals,
The sound that resonate with every art,
The sound that directly speaks to the heart.

The sound of my people moves the world,
The sound of my people fills me with joy,
The sound of my people will be in every spoken word.

There's something organic about this sound,
Around the world the nature is filled with vibration,
Everything in motion, then gravity keeps it on the ground,
This is a sound for every generation.

THE WOLF AND THE MOON

The cow jumped over the moon.
The little dog laughed at me,
But the wolf only smiled.
'Be gone', I yelled.

I've seen things that a human should see not.
A sea hauling at the moon
A moon calming waves.
Voices crying in hell
What have you done dear friend?

Now that the secret is out.
The cow jumped over the moon.
The little dog laughed at me
But the wolf only smiled.

Be off with you, I yelled.
For the demons are welcoming me home on the full moon.

The World Has Its Fragrance

The world has its fragrance
O people, smell it and absorb it

We do not belong
To some other planet
The world on mother-earth
Has no equal

This world is ours
Our ancestors'
And their ancestors'

We belong to the world
The world belongs to us

We have to long for the world
Our longing should be strong for the world

Learn to live in the world
Live to learn from the world

For sake not, forget not
No one forbids you

O people, smell it and absorb it
The world has its fragrance

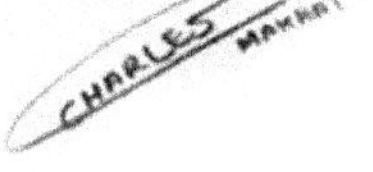

THERE IS A THE REASON

I grew up in Africa for a season,
I came to oozy for a reason,
I daily fulfil my mission,
I already had permission.

There is a reason why I daily sing,
I have something valuable to bring,
Sometimes in front of a shiny ring,
And people have a great wedding.

There's a reason why I write,
To give you light through the night,
It doesn't matter if you're black or white,
There's a thin line between wrong and right.

There's a reason why I dance,
I'm declaring that there's another chance,
Stop worrying about your finance,
You can go through every circumstance.

THERE THE DEVIL THAT STOLE MY HEART

When she danced by the ocean, I felt Hell breeze all over my hair.
It loomed all around me.
I opened the door to my heart for her and made love on the vain that
pumped blood of trust.
As innocent as she looked, like an angel, she was a devil for my heart.

She gently kissed me
I was a Kassie
She took control of every limb
She aimed for the soul,
Thank GOD I had already sent it back to heaven,
So she settled for the heart
She slowly told me how much of evil she was,
Heart paid no mind.

She ran wild against the desert sand
The wind blew through her hair like a comb
Building castles from dust
Slaying any against her wishes.
And as I watched from a far, I knew she already had won my heart,
But
Never my soul.

TO BEAR A SOUL

If I tell you I love you at this moment
With a look in my eye that testifies

Know am standing before you naked
For I bear my soul in earnest

Like Moses' bare footedness on holy ground
You ask me to tap deep to my confines

How do I say this without shaking a bit?
Be tossed to and fro like a leaf

If I tell you I love you this minute
In the midst of all nature observing
Let it be known I stood in truthfulness
Mirroring contents held in my heart
I wish to find the best words to tell you how
All draped in the best of chosen wears
Yet love is but a feeling

You cannot touch but feel its tone
I stand before you naked

The windows of my soul, open
See deep within the contents

Be lost in the sea of my emotions
Like a vessel sail in my waters

Lower your anchor to my bed
Within me you're in safest of streams
Yes, I love you beyond these uttered words

TO EACH HAS ITS OWN

Some are good at playing chess.
Some sing beautifully.

Some make the same old joke,
Funny how they still laugh out loud.

Shame my family name once, but never again
Shame on me or you, it's a win, win situation.
I guess it depends on the GODS.

To each has its own
A gift you carry through this earth
A gift born within hands folded
How can one learn?
Cemeteries' filled with one.
To each has its own and by God no one can take that from you

A gifted hand deep in the heart
A seed will one day be an oak tree
A flowing screams lead water to the sea
You're the only power
The controller of your life.

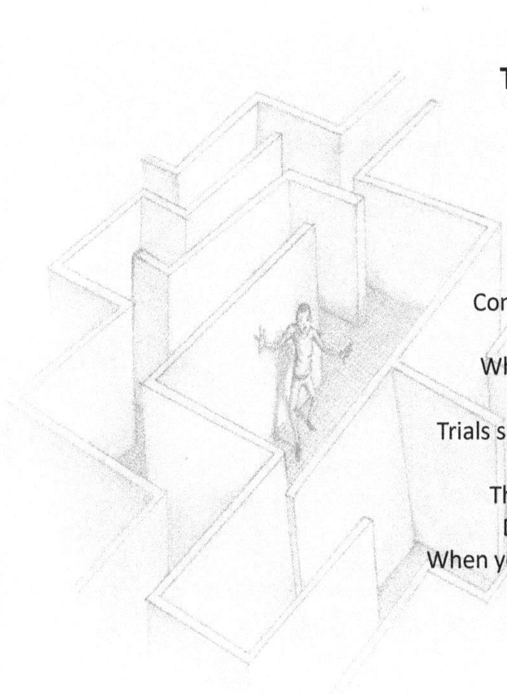

TRIAL AND ERROR

Trial and error
Is on trial
For guiding the lost
To the dead end
Of a maze of choices.
Constructed by the architects
Of society.
Where an error in judgment
Is always costly.
Trials seem to be an insurmountable
Mountain
Thrust upon us unwanted.
Do not quail with terror
When you are asked to make a change
In your routine.
Being shown the error
Of your ways
Is a lesson
Never learned.

Twist and Turn

The dog goes right-round chasing its own tail.
The cow graze on the green grass,
Politician can't charge VAT on that.

The dog is loyal to its master like the 80's slave
Nowadays White boys are sitting ducks on the land of black lions.
Nowadays politicians charge VAT on everything and blame apartheid

Run Billy old boy for they are coming.
Run as fast as you can, head for the hills
Better the beast of the jungle then them,
For they will eat you raw, and sell your soul to the devil.
Run Billy old boy for the dog you once owned has bitten off the hand you fed it
with.
Run as fast as you can, head for the hills for the hills have eyes.
The dog goes right-round chasing its own tail, coming back as it is.
The cow graze on the green grass,
Politician can't charge VAT on that,
Grass that is.

UNSOLICITED

Here comes the cattle ringing a bell.
And once again I was thinking of red wine and sweet
roses.
Alone on top of the roof I start to script.
Alone as always.

I guess I am in touch with such motion
Here…..Here full moon,
Shine your light on me.

Here…..Here shooting star,
I could really use a wish right now.
It's just you and me
The mood is right
The wine is matured
It has aged right
Yet I am still alone

Petals of the rain flow in from the sky
Should I wear a rain coat?
Should I grab a hold of an umbrella?
Or,
Should I let it cleanse all my sins away?

WHAT WE TALKED ABOUT WHEN WE SPOKE IN SILENCE

Eyes never lost sight
Hands longed each other
Feet beneath the table kissed

I knew her birth mark
She knew my scars
Her husband was a best friend of mine
My wife was a friend of hers'

I couldn't help, but notice,
My wife spoke the same language with my friend that I spoke with her friend.
Their eyes also never lost sight.
I wonder whose feet touched me.

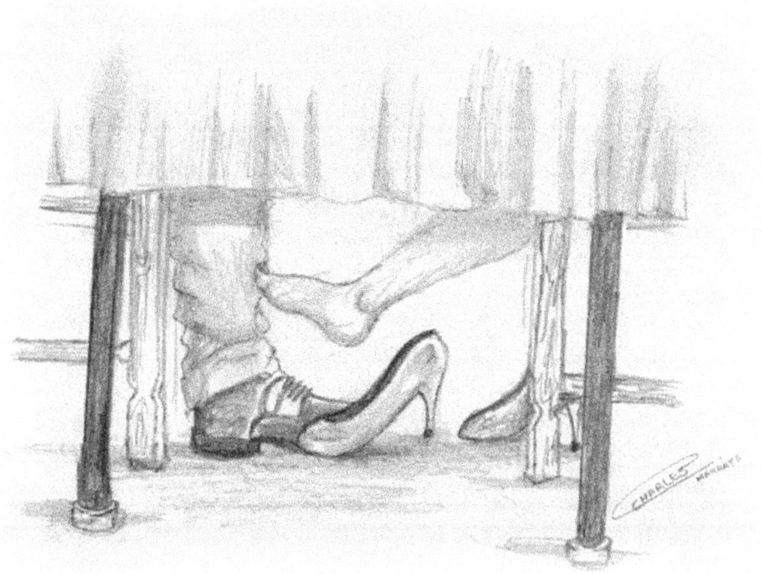

WHERE IS HOME?

I've packed
And unpacked
Far too long
The path has been crooked
The Miles long
So I search
So I seek
A home for my jazzy
A home for me
Not a home
Where I'll be for awhile
Not a home where I'll have to leave before
Long
A home for a long time
A home to settle down
A home to sit and watch the spiders
Weaved their cobwebs all along
A home to watch the years fly by
And top tell stories,
Some of truth, some stretched by lies
Some places I've given up by choice
Some I was told to leave
Where I had no voice
No choice
Told to move on
Left them in the past
But the memories live on
I've had a few places
Here and there
Where I have lived for awhile
But permanency was not there
So where is home
I ask of you
Where is a home where my dreams of settling
down will come true?

WOLF BREATH

The wolf he breaths heavy
Deep breaths in frustration
Totally riled up and ready
For the final confrontation

As he looks to the moon
A reflection of this earth
Howling loudly in frustration
In anger for all that is worth

His partner caught and caged
Savaged by the beast more
Powerful, human and wolf
Unique this thing for sure

As he howled at the moon
Into the night sky he cried
Bitter salty tears in his eyes
On the night that she died
Now this most beautiful beast

Left here alone in this world
This last breath of sadness
Breaths life to the afterworld.

WONDERS OF THE TRAVELER

I wonder where the God they spoke off, for so many years is
I wonder if I'll die alone, with no-one to care for me
I am a traveler on this world.
On my journey I have seen a lot.
On my journey there is a lot to be seen
Every time when my heart ask of the heavens I ignore
Every time when my heart ask me of God I say "he lives in me"
It takes some time to master these roads GOD knows how
long.
GOD knows them all
I have danced with nude woman on the sea shore.
I have watched the sunset with someone's wife.

Tasted devils water
Sang lullaby with the angels.
I am a traveler on this world.
I have seen a lot.
There is a lot to be seen,
Yet I wonder
Yet curiosity kills me in the city of lotus eaters

Why was I born?
For we are all travelers in this world
Seeking what is known not
Seeking our path back
From dust we came and to dust we shall return,
But I still wonder the purpose of it all.

~THE END~

Swansong {closing poem}

I have seen this world with toddler's eyes
I have crawled on these harsh lands with my knees both as a child and an adult,
Seen many of my kind.
Life is a battlefield, we all get scared.
It crazy how we are all connected yet turn blind eye when one is in need of hope, I
thought we war as a nation but I guess I was wrong, it's every man for himself out
here.

It is true after all, that you cannot see the frame when you're inside the picture.
Who are we to paint each other wrong whilst pausing for the picture?
Who are we to mislead with words but less action?
Writers or poets?

Authors or observers and philosophers?
If so, then the question lingers, is you is or is you not, the same as when you
escape the womb?
Aren't we all trying to be someone or something?
Every wolf needs to howl at the full moon every once in a while,
Let howl as a pack.

BIOGRAPH
POETS/ ARTIST

<u>Bhekumuzi Kubheka</u>
Bhekumuzi Kubheka is the AUTHOR and creator of Poetry Movement series Books of Anthologies featuring various artist from around the world.

Born and bred in Durban, this vibrant young writer has published his works with lot of online publishers in South Africa. He mostly write about what meets the eye and beyond, he has also wrote stunning short stories for magazines and is set to publish a compilation of short stories in the near future. His goal now is for his work to move abroad, and be published international.

You can find his books on amazon.com or lulu.com and other online shops, you can also grab ahold of them in bookshops around Africa

 Alternative contact details are as follows:
Website: http://poetrymovement.wordpress.com
E-mail: bhekikubheka@outlook.com
Facebook page: Poetry Movement
Google plus: bhekikubheka50@gmail.com
Instar: @bhekikubheka50/
Twitter: @bhekikubheka50

Gracia Asian Poet Gernale
Gracia Gernale
A Filipino born in Bulla, sorsogon
Parents Mr. & Mrs. Felizardo Gernale
A graduate of two degrees: Bachelor of Arts degree in AB Mas communication
Bachelor of laws
Pres. & Gen. Manager of MTNC cargo sea air express
CEO KMTNC Trading ISO Tank & Int'l. Movers Inc.
Alternative contact details are as follows:
Facebook page: league of international writers and authors

John Smallshaw
John smallshaw an ex drug addict, ex homeless. Now happily married,
Link to some of his great work johnsmallshaw.com
This awesome poet goes on to mention a great house of St. Barnabas a charity that helps the homeless back into employment of how they had helped him when his feet were dangling
Alternative contact details are as follows:
Websites: johnsmallshaw.com
            : http://pantechniconpoet.wordpress.com
        : http://linesofjohn.com
E-mail: recordpublicrelations@gmail.com
Facebook: facebook.com/jsmallshaw
Twitter: @jsirony

Mark Olynyk

Mark olynyk is a poet with a philosophical bent. In 1977, Mark published his first poem in "left Wing"; an alternative school paper. This event set off a chain reaction of poetry; that continues to this day. His poems have appeared in anthologies and literary journals, such as, The Prairie journal, Canadian writer's Journal, The Pen wood Review, nomad's choir and peace & Freedom. In 1997 mark's first poetry chapbook, the interior sea, was published by plowman. In 2012, his first full length poetry book, written in stone, was released by Friesen Press.

Patrick Daniel Read

45years old disabled army vet from the United States father of three.
He has more than 30years of experience in poetry
Some of his books like CHANGING THE WORLD FOR THE BETTER THROUGH POETRY/ can be accessed on amazon.com and lulu.com
Alternative contact details are as follows:
E-mail: patrickread@hotmail.com
Yahoo! Messenger: philscoach
Website: http://www.lulu.com/spotlight/spread71
Facebook: facebook.com/Patrick.d.read

Percy Shozi

Also known as (MQO) a founder of Heart to Art Organisation in Melbourne, Australia.

He had performed in the presence of South African president and prime ministers in Australia

He has published two books called 'I AM SOLD' and 'WINGS OF AN EAGLE" available on retailing stores

 Alternative contact details are as follows:

Blog: "power of poetry" http://mqoshozi.blogspot.com

Website: http://percyspoems.com

E-mail: percyshozi@gmail.com

Phumla Xuza Khanyile

Phumla Khanyile is first and foremost a mother of three, a grandmother, a daughter, and a sister. To some, she is a reliable friend. She studied Journalism at the Tshwane University of Technology in Pretoria, South Africa; looking back, she says this was her then misdirected heed to the love she has always had for writing. Her ventures into writing poetry are recent. She calls them her 'means of self-release from emotions of things experienced personally or observed'. Her poems are heart-felt, and Phumla hopes they appeal to other emotional souls out there, talk healing, and preach understanding to those who have the need.

 Phumla' s work features in a number of poetry groups on Facebook and in the year 2015 she has been published in three poetry anthologies: Cupid (published in Zimbabwe in February) Letters from Africa (published in Uganda in May); Out of the Storm: Love should hurt (published in US) and recently Poets

Against Inequality (Published in Italy).   In the Month of September, her book Love Notes hit the shores of Mzansi (South Africa) and braced Amazon pages. Recently, her work was selected to feature in the 2016 Nomads Choir Poetry Journal published in New York.

What distinguishes Phumla's work is her style of writing and tone. She intentionally writes with the aim to evoke strong emotions through her pieces. To obtain a copy of her own poetry compilation – Love Notes – published here in South Africa in September 2015,

Alternative contact details are as follows:

Email: liliespebbles@gmail.com

Twitter: https://twitter.com/khanyile_p

Facebook: facebook.com/phumla

<u>Rochish Mon</u>

Rochishmon is a self-employed entrepreneur at Chennai, originating from Vijayawada, India

He writes poetry in English, Telugu, Tamil, Sanskrit languages.

His English poems have reached 108 countries and have received more than 3, 00,000 views.

Rchish Mon's recently released English anthology LET US UNDERSTAND THE DAWNS can be obtained at www.authorspressbook.com/index.php

In the literature of the language Telugu he holds 3 records…

He introduced one line poems in Telugu language for the first time.

He introduced the first anthology of poetry on the internet in the language of Telugu.

He introduced Ghazal for the first time on the internet in the language of Telugu.
He wrote Telugu Ghazal in prescribed Ethnic-Bihar's for the 1st time.
He introduced proper Rubaayees in Telugu for the first time.
He introduced Persian poetry from Qat'a into the language of Telugu.
He introduced Rubaayee and Qat'a in the language of Tamil.

Shane Flynn

Shane Flynn, modern Irish poet, is a unique modern poet from Dublin, Ireland. His simplistic style of varied poetry is easy on both the eyes and the mind.
Poetry created from within his heart.
Alternative contact details are as follows
E-mail: shanea38@gmail.com
Facebook page: modern Irish Poet

Smiso SlashFire Sokhela

Smiso was born in Umlazi Township and grew up in an informal settlement called Canaan in Clare estate just outside Durban.
His book is called 'Wordography with a Pen'
He's the founder of numerous poetry societies, such as bold new poets and helps groom young aspiring writers by sourcing new performance platforms and facilitating workshops.
Alternative contact details are as follows
Facebook page: slashfirepoetry
Website: www.slashfirepoetry.webs.com
Instagram: @slashfirepoetry

Zama Dlamini
Zama s Dlamini is an artist, a leader that is passionate about art.
A poet, writer and motivational speaker.
Graduated for leadership at world changers, facilitated for life skills, self-development in high schools
Changing lives of the youth.
Alternative contact details are as follows
Facebook page: Zama Dlamini
E-mail: zamadlamini2012@gmail.com

www.ingramcontent.com/pod-product-compliance
Lightning Source LLC
Chambersburg PA
CBHW061035050726
47592CB00004B/1455